Pr

Search "Michael Chamblain Dunks"

"This guy wants to know if Keith is available," I told Michael. "What do I tell him?"

"He probably can't afford Keith," Michael replied. "Who is he reppin'?" "He represents...some team in the Euro league?"

I gotta pick up an overseas basketball directory. "Is he legit?" Michael asked.

"Hold on, Mike. Gimmie a minute to check the full message." The same message that sat in my inbox for two days. "I'll look him up."

Michael, a certified NBA Agent, contacted me two years ago because he wanted a public speaking refresher course. Already an accomplished lecturer, he was looking for additional tips, and he'd heard that I train professional athletes. Michael enjoys holding workshops for those interested in sports management, and teaches a class whenever his schedule permits. Finding the opportunity is rare, with a list of duties that include a board post at his alma mater, coursework at law school, sports agent responsibilities, and owning partial stake in Bnei Herzliya, one of the top pro basketball clubs in Israel.

Michael scheduled a meeting to learn more about my services. "Did you hoop?" I asked during our consult-ation.

"A little," Michael responded.

"Well, I normally work with pro players...but I got time," I sniffed. A YouTube search revealed footage of my newest client, all 5'7 of him, jumping out of the gym. (Search "Michael Chamblain Dunks.")

"You kinda downplayed your basketball career, huh, Mike?"

Michael played point guard for the Berlin Baskets, Lok Vernau, and the Peru Metro Allstars. NBA Champion point guard and former Cavs head coach Tyronn Lue once expressed to Michael how a few more inches of height would have given him a legitimate shot at playing in the NBA.

The rep who was looking for Keith's agent initially contacted me, so I played a major role in the business deal. (I relayed an email.) I got the inquiry because Michael is a member of my firm Pro Speak for Athletes. Our speakers bureau is a group of pro athletes who work the public speaking circuit. Within days, Mike negotiated a deal that sent Keith to play for a club in Argentina.

Before connecting with me, Michael was already working the public speaking circuit, delivering workshops on college campuses. He just wanted to hone his speech skills. To be an even better public speaker. This, I would learn, is how he handles all work objectives. He has a methodical approach to rehearsing speech presentations, evaluating pro players, and mentoring prospective sports agents. Now we team up to host a Sports Management Academy, and these notes are an extension of Michael's workshops.

Dr. Yardan W. Shabazz

SPORTS MANAGEMENT NOTES FROM MICHAEL CHAMBLAIN

Pro Player. Sports Agent.
Owner. with Yardan Shabazz

I met Maverick Carter, LeBron James' business manager, on May 27, 2018. It was the same night the Cleveland Cavaliers defeated the Boston Celtics in the Eastern Conference Final. Jay Carter, a mutual friend, introduced us. We dined at our friend Nick Verano's Boston restaurant Strip. Soon, I was sharing a table with Maverick, Boston Celtics assistant manager Mike Zarren, professional ice hockey defenseman P.K. Subban, and World Cup alpine ski racer Lindsey Vonn. We recapped the game, conversing like sports analysts. I was fixated on Maverick's jacket. Maverick wore a Liverpool F.C. jacket, representing the professional football club that competes in the English Premier League. He secured a deal that earned LeBron James partial stake in that team, expanding their overseas exposure. That jacket was his brand. The conversation switched to menu items. My thoughts switched to brokering. If I could manage player contracts with a ball club, I could propose an arrangement for partial ownership. That was the night I decided to become a co-owner.

Pursuing partial ownership became a new career goal, but my sports agent duties keep me busy. They're like having an on-call job. The role of the sports agent has been glamorized (Shropshire, K. and Davis, T., 2008). The entertainment industry has redefined the role, making it a stock character.

Recurring tropes include the fictional sports agent in an expensive suit. Vintage sports car. Engaged in a heated cell phone conversation. These character traits are just as common as the ones found in every sports team movie (the boy who wears a cowboy hat, the kid with glasses, the tomboy, and the drunk coach who sobers up before the championship game).

Real-life sports agents do earn perks from their profession, but their jobs extend beyond driving custom cars and negotiating mega-deals. It is important for anyone interested in working as a sports agent to become fully aware of the day-to-day responsibilities. Sports management is a demanding and exciting career field in which you can be responsible for a list of duties that range from pro athlete management to accounting. Business management, financial literacy, human resource planning, and media relations are all essential elements of sports management. These elements make up the foundation to becoming a sports agent, but you can start laying the groundwork today.

1 GROUNDWORK

Anyone seeking a career in sports management is most likely a sports fan. Sports fans are already familiar with sports league rules and trends. However, a more diligent sports agent will become familiar with business trends in several leagues, not just the sport where he or she will attempt to land clients. For instance, I was contacting companies two years ago to inform them about a rising talent, Naomi Osaka. I explained to ad executives how this tennis player would soon be one of the tennis world's more popular figures. Endorsement reps were not convinced. Still, I was happy to advocate for a friend. (Naomi eventually earned the ranking of the number one tennis player in the world, and now her agent fields calls from those same endorsement reps.)

In order to become a certified sports agent, an agent should at least hold a bachelor's degree. Thankfully, the popularity of sports agency has influenced more schools to offer a degree in sport management. In addition, sports agents are also encouraged to earn a master's degree in either public relations or marketing. Business management is another major to consider. (Top tier sports agencies typically feature agents who have also attended law school, giving them a competitive edge in player contract negotiations.) Next, an agent must pass a league sports agent exam, which is normally held once every year. The sports agent exam can cost between $600 to $1,200, and agents are required to pay fees in order to maintain certification.

Just as important as getting certified is laying the groundwork, and it involves volunteering hours as a team manager, assistant coach, or trainer. Students interested in a career in sports management should be developing relationships with the school's sports teams. Like...now. Ask the basketball coach if he or she needs someone to record stats, carry equipment, wash jerseys, tutor players, or rebound during warm-ups.

Some of those spots are already taken by other future sports agents. Therefore, ask the field hockey coach, football coach, wrestling team, volleyball squad, baseball team, swimming coach, or track club. Working with a school's sports team will lay the groundwork for a sports management career, helping a future sports agent develop relationships with athletes. It is the most reliable opportunity to network, and it helps to be aware of developments occurring in other sports areas besides the ones you enjoy watching.

2 TRAINER

I have been all about sports, since, always. Basketball has been my favorite. Excelling as a player has granted me access to play in college and travel the world. There was more to learn about the business of sports, so I stayed connected after I played my last game. I started training. Guards. Big men. I had a knack for coaching. Even better, I had a knack for fostering relationships.

Personal training kept me close to the game. Coaching professional athletes provided fulfillment. It is a personal reward to help other players achieve their goals and reach the next steps in their respective careers. Ultimately, one of my mentees asked me if I could represent him in contract talks. This switch from his trainer to player representative started my sports agent career.

I have negotiated contracts in more than 10 countries, meeting with some savvy professional ball club decision-makers. I hold meetings with these decision- makers in order to promote my clients and negotiate contracts. Not long ago, I was reading defenses, feeding my bigs in the post and drafting plays on the sideline. Now I'm reading, redlining, and drafting deals. No longer do I study game film. I study contracts.

3 DUTIES

An agent is responsible for locating jobs, connecting with teams in need of their clients' skills. This requires a player's rep who is adept at promotion and coordinating campaigns with a public relations firm. The goal is to market a player- yet another sports agent duty. Once talks between agent and team management begin, a contract is soon proposed. At this point in the negotiation, an agent has played a role as his or her client's mediator, counselor, public relations coordinator, and brand manager. This is how a sports agent becomes an integral part of a professional athlete's inner circle.

Professional athletes consider teammates, members of their coaching staff, and agents as their most loyal allies. Agents advise, mentor, and negotiate on behalf of pro athletes and, in many cases, become a pro athlete's most trusted friend. For those services, an agent can charge an athlete in a variety of ways. An agent can take a percentage from an athlete's earning, which is typically 2- 4% in the NBA. It's 10% standard overseas. At this rate, if an agent brokers a player's yearly salary range at $475,000, the agent's commission is almost $10,000. An agent can also charge an hourly rate, flat fee, or arrange charges by a combination of these means.

A sports agent's work is challenging, with newcomers learning firsthand just how many years of networking is required before reaping financial rewards. For instance, some agents have fostered relationships that go back to their client's middle school career. If you love sports, you will enjoy building a rapport. You will also love negotiating the best deals for your clients. Be aware that the field is stressful and competitive. In fact, the business of sports agency includes fierce competition and unethical behavior, with agents stealing clients (Shropshire, K. and Davis, T., 2008). The competition between agents continues to affect the market. Luckily, there is room for the next generation, since a sports agent is now a facet of every competitive athletic level. For example, there are just as many sports agents attending amateur tennis matches as there are agents sitting courtside at basketball games.

4 PREPARE TO MANAGE...AND MORE

Sports agents manage the terms of their client's involvement on the court, field, or television studio. I am often asked by workshop attendees, "What is your day like?" Certain parts of the job I do every day. Talking with clients, checking box scores, and constantly seeking new deals and opportunities. With so many responsibilities involved, you can never truly know what your role will be tomorrow. Be flexible. The job can be exhilarating if you're adventurous and love taking on challenges in the sports industry. Or, you could seek another position with a sports agency, working as an accountant, returning phone calls, emails, and negotiating deals via fax.

Be prepared to handle several duties as a sports agent, especially after landing clients. Landing clients is every agent's goal, but the work does not end there. My list of responsibilities expands with each new client. You must be available at all times, and there is no such thing as a job that isn't yours. There will be days when you have to carry out non-sports related errands and activities, such as providing updates for family members. It can be your responsibility to call a client's family member to provide news on day-to-day traveling affairs.

You will be tasked with providing information on your client's health, or you may have to call a spouse to check up on the birth of the couple's newborn. A sports agent will often be called upon to provide transportation from a club, airport, or gym. One client may need branding consultation, while another may request relationship advice. You want to be a sports agent? Be prepared to act as agent, errand-runner, medical liaison, travel planner, Uber driver, brand consultant, and confidant. Be the sports agent who performs these duties and you will increase the chance of keeping the clients you signed.

Sports agents spend time creating relationships and establishing trust with players, and this is a process that begins when players are still in their teens. I know sports agents who began fostering relationships with players during summer youth camps.

Unfortunately, this relationship does not guarantee a player's loyalty. Your clientele will mostly consist of teenagers. Young people who will hear other agents promise contracts worth "twice as much money" than the one you negotiated. It's that easy for a rival sports agent to persuade your client to leave your management team. The sports agency field is not only time consuming, it is competitive and stressful. Sports agents can devote years to a professional athlete and lose that client to another agent with one chance meeting. It happens. It can happen. They can leave.

5 MOTIVES

A variety of personalities make up this industry. Learning who you want to work with is important. Some clients will need you more than others. I'll get called more often by one client, asked by another to check on a relative with much more frequency, and I may even have to pick up a birthday gift for a player's mother. It's part of the job, and it can leave me with little time to pursue other ventures (like seeking partial ownership of a ball club).

As someone who has a passion for assisting, I chose to run for my town's School Committee. It is one of several initiatives I employ to help the youth and community. My involvement in local town government was not planned. In fact, the role of a School Committee member or Town Council member in most small towns is not financially rewarding. Landing a spot with either group won't exactly push me into a higher tax bracket. Nor is my quest to attend and graduate from law school. My mission to help those around me is the bigger picture. The biggest picture.

Initially, I wanted to give back to the community because I felt extremely honored to work and compete among such great businessmen. Sure, most people are huge fans of NBA players. But I saw the NBA and the entire sports industry as a wonderful place for anyone just lucky enough to have first-hand access. Building a network has landed me connections with decision-makers for several sports organizations. Eventually, my reputation as an ambitious agent grew. It soon led to business competition with "high power" sports agents from CAA, Wasserman, and Excel, the sports industry's largest agencies. On the other hand, it didn't take long to realize not many of the gentlemen I was competing against looked like me. It was then I knew I had to help students realize what it would take to gain entry into the sports industry. The hard part is mapping out a traditional plan of action, because I know my path to sports agency was unconventional.

I was aware of my professional basketball career timeline. I also knew my stint as a trainer would lead to another role. Evolving into a sports agent was a natural transition, and I was already familiar with potential clientele.

Players who were seeking my guidance with contractual negotiations were already professionals. They did not need my help to get to the pro level. Instead, they needed someone who would be honest, sedulous, and always have their best interests in mind. This is the same approach I take with all of my clients. Years of experience as a professional basketball player gives me an advantage in this area, because I still think like a pro player. My other advantage in the area of contactual negotiations includes everything I learn in law school. Law school coursework gives me an edge in the business of sports. Everyone needs an edge, especially in sports business.

Working as an agent has introduced me to the corruption and greed involved in sports agency. By holding sports management workshops, I may be able to steer some future agents away from the dark practices that plague the sports world.

Earning a Sport Management degree is the right start. Earning a law degree is the right leverage. Even though law school is a big commitment, the dedication required to complete coursework will prove advantageous for an agent's career. Study business. Become a marketing student. Learn basic principles of law. These courses will help you develop skills necessary to becoming a contract-savvy sports agent. Continue to learn. Read sports publications and books to stay ahead in the sports industry. Start now with your groundwork so you can be fully equipped to begin managing clients. Enroll in those marketing classes so you can

Michael Chamblain

learn how to create a unique list of services.

6 SERVICES

I'm grateful to be one of few privileged individuals to connect on a business level with major sports franchises. In fact, I have been lucky enough to play with pro athletes, coach pro players, train athletes, work in management, and now act as co-owner of a professional basketball club. Now I have clients who are more like family, and I care for them beyond the court. Success for them means success for my business. However, it all ends one day. It ends for everyone, leaving us facing an uncharted path. This is why a sports agent is responsible for tailoring career transition options for every client, which is not easy.

Young pro athletes are convinced they will play forever. Older pro athletes have waited too long to begin learning a second career skill set. A sports agent must be prepared to foster non-athletic development, because career transition from sports to the business world can be challenging. This is where you can separate yourself from other sports agents: offer career transition services.

Convince professional athletes you will work to earn them the best contracts. Make them trust the fact you will negotiate endorsement deals on their behalf. Help them understand just how much you will network, market, and brand in order to increase their stock. You will include this in your pitch to potential clients...and they will field calls from dozens of other sports agents who will promise them the same services.

What will you offer players that will make you stand out from your competitors? Define your role as a career transition specialist. Hire one or become one. Add to your sports agency pitch that you will be working for your client after he or she has stepped away from the field or court. Explain to your potential clients that you will help them learn other job skills to keep them marketable long after their playing days end.

For instance, a game analyst is one of the most sought after post-career positions for former professional athletes. Unfortunately, many pro athletes wait until the end of their playing days to begin preparing for post-career work. Be that sports agent who acts as a career transition specialist, holding speech classes for your clients in an attempt to prepare them for sports analyst job auditions. Sign them up for classes in acting, finance, and public speaking. Your goal should be managing pro players' contract negotiations, and preparing them for a career after sports by providing life skills management.

7 CONTRACTS

It is critical to research a country before negotiating an overseas contract. A once-in-a-lifetime opportunity can reap benefits, with your client getting free room and board, travel arrangements, and a meal plan. You can land your player on a squad that is in dire need of his or her skills, and there are perks that come with it-starring on a team and building a fan base that will attract attention throughout the globe. However, a sports agent must first research the team, coach, city, culture, and political climate. For instance, a lucrative contract is not worth sending someone to a war-torn country.

An agent keeps an account of current events the same way he checks game stats. In addition, maintaining communication is more important with international players. It is easy to build and maintain relationships with clients who are stateside. You can see them. International players are in different time zones, with game and cultural events occurring when you're sleeping. I often visit clients in Israel, which is very important to players. Most players do not have family members who can make the expensive trip. For most clients, an agent is their only visible support.

Getting through customs at Tel Aviv can sometimes be difficult, especially with someone who has plenty of passport stamps. I have flown to see clients in Dubai and Turkey, so it is common for my passport to raise a red flag at customs. ("Why are you here when you were just visiting that country?") On the other hand, customs does not deter an agent from enjoying a perk to signing a player overseas: another visit to a beautiful city.

Tel Aviv looks like Miami. The beaches are just as scenic and the weather is comparable. Business includes lunch with my client, meeting with his coach, and dinner with the team's general managers. An agent must maintain these ties, since the organization always needs another great player. This places more pressure on your client to perform well, because managers will contact his agent when there is interest for another player in a different position. There is also the possibility another club will seek to purchase my client's contract once the season reaches end, which is a likely scenario that can occur on an entirely different time zone when his agent is back stateside-and asleep.

8 REWARD

Working as a professional basketball player allowed me to travel to places I would have never dreamt to visit. I saw the "Blonde Bombshells" in Stockholm, experienced German culture, and stood at the site of the initial fall of the Berlin Wall. My pro career even afforded me a visit to Machu Picchu in Peru. It was culture shock for a person who grew up in Randolph, Massachusetts, and I consider myself lucky.

Professional athletes are fueled by the adrenaline rush that comes with playing in front of thousands. Coaching provides just as big of a rush. My heart pumps just as hard when I'm on the sideline, living and dying with every play, and then preparing for the next one.

I still enjoy that adrenaline rush. Nowadays, I experience it via clients. I feel their ups and downs with wins and losses. Not all of my clients are on the same team. Still, we exist in the same family, sending well wishes for brothers, sisters, and cousins to excel. Sometimes, those family members face off on opposing teams. In sports, this is part of the business. In life? There are days when two of your clients are playing against each other.

The business scenario where two of your clients are playing each other can be stressful, but I am pretty relaxed. I want the team that needs the win more to win. That way they both have longer seasons and earn more money. (The most stress that I endure when watching two clients play involves praying they both enjoy an injury-free game.)

Sports agent duties can certainly be as stressful as any other job. Your primary concern will be to manage your clients' professional and personal matters. Yet, the perks include travel and the excitement that comes with the outlook of a new season. The most successful pro athletes rely on hard- working sports agents to manage their businesses-their brands...their airport transportation. It's part of the job, combining business with personal affairs. Stick with this long enough, and you'll achieve a rewarding balance.

9 OWNERSHIP

Professional sports team owners make up a very exclusive club (Michael, 2008). Gaining ownership is difficult; even for the super-rich. A team's board of directors conducts a vetting process that determines whether a potential owner will be both financially and mentally fit. This process includes an extensive background check. Billionaires have been rejected. Those who gain ownership of a pro team typically serve as the CEO of a large manufacturer or corporation. Very few minorities are in that club.

Minorities who have a bank account large enough to buy a professional sports team are usually superstar professional athletes. I am a rare minority. I co-own a professional basketball team. Bnei Herzliya of Israel. I was not a superstar. Not a billionaire CEO. I studied the business of ownership.

Black people are not conditioned to consider "ownership." Many of us are content with good benefits. While the NBA features teams stacked with Black professional basketball players, pro sports do not feature many Blacks who are prepared to seek ownership. I trained in order to become a professional basketball player. Passed an exam in order to become a certified agent. Studied management to become an owner.

My father is West Indian. He was born in Haiti, moving to America as a young adult. He came for education. For the opportunity to live a better life. He was part of a large migration of Haitians who moved to the Boston area.

My mother is from the south. Born in Colerain. It is a town in Bertie County, North Carolina. She relocated to Boston at the age of 18, joining aunts who left Colerain years prior. She came for education. They both sought refuge. My father escaping political oppression and poverty. My mother getting away from the farm. My parents modeled a work ethic, one that advocates gaining secure employment. My work ethic evolved into entrepreneurship.

Jeff Adrien is a power forward who can also man the middle. Possessing a soft stroke from beyond the arc, he's the type of big who can stretch a floor. We were introduced by a mutual acquaintance who told me the 6'7 professional basketball player was looking for an agent, and Jeff and I are from the same area in Massachusetts. I met with Jeff in Boston and watched him work out, so I could evaluate his basketball acumen. Agents can watch online videos to assess a player's talent, but those are posts both the player and coach want you to see. Watching a player workout up close offers the chance to see other dimensions of his skills set, personality, and work ethic. Highlight reels do not reveal a player's will. His attitude.

We finalized a contract afterwards, which established Jeff as my client. Since he played for teams in the NBA, Europe, and China, Jeff garnered interest from several Israeli pro basketball clubs. Team managers asked about my newly signed client's availability, but the Bnei Herzliya coach offered a plan that would best utilize Jeff's talents. Bnei Herzliya plays in the Israeli Premier League and was competing in the FIBA Europe Cup. It is a city that features beautiful weather and a visitor-friendly community. Plus, it is a short drive to Tel Aviv, one of the most vivacious cities in the world. He signed on August 22, 2016.

Being selected to the Israeli League All-Star game, Jeff's first season was a success. He enjoyed the team and grew more fond of the city, so he signed again the following season. Jeff and I negotiated a two-year contract extension with Bnei Herzliya on August 24, 2017. My client then enjoyed an even more productive second season, finishing as the Israeli League's fifth-leading scorer. By May 2018, the second season was nearing a close, and we had leverage to opt out and renegotiate another contract.

By this time, my client had been named the Israeli League Player of the Month for the games he played in March, recording career highs in points and rebounds. At this point, Jeff grew so comfortable with the city of Herzliya that he considered moving to the city upon retirement. On July 3, 2018, Jeff signed a three-year contract extension.

I profited from having a good relationship with Bnei Herzliya. I brokered deals on Jeff's behalf that eventually led to a long-term deal. He was putting up impressive numbers, and he enjoyed the organization. I approached management and expressed interest in ownership. They were skeptical. Jeff is my client, so they were worried about conflict of interest. Would I be effective as club decision-maker and Jeff's agent? Meetings were held to discuss my duality. Since we have a good history, the ownership discussions were conducted as smoothly as Jeff's contract negotiations. The conversations with board members were equally positive.

They approved my offer. Then my lawyers met with their lawyers to broker the deal. It was a 4-month process, and I received news the board approved the deal in October 2018. I officially became co-owner of Bnei Herzliya in November 2018.

Now it's my turn to brand. I brokered a deal to own partial stake in a professional ball club. Marketing this overseas team became priority. Thus, it requires ingenuity to make the brand grow. There are merchandise sales goals, summer basketball workshops, and podcasts to schedule. Collaborating with a television network is ideal, but that involves finding an on-air slot best suited to our team. Getting a game broadcasted here in the states would be a major marketing accomplishment, but the time zone difference between here and Bnei Herzliya makes finding the right time slot difficult.

In addition to those responsibilities, I have a roster to fill. This requires searching the market for talented players. It only takes one key roster addition to alter the culture of a team. For instance, finding the right ball handler can augment the offense. Signing a shutdown defender can propel the team's defensive unit. I am evaluating talent to find that guy. I am searching to find both of those guys.

When I locate that talent, I will sign him to play for Bnei Herzliya, but not as my client. That is how I separate my duties as co-owner and agent. The duties attached with co-ownership -filling out the roster, discussing television deals, and selling merchandise-are necessary to make the ball club grow. Signing players as clients are necessary to make my sports agency grow. There is an advantage to having experience as both a professional player and sports agent. I am familiar with the nuances of the game, so I can easily determine the right fit for a player's skills. I also understand know how to approach a player who may need representation.

There is an advantage to being exposed to ideas shared by prominent sports industry figures like Maverick Carter. That dinner at Strip gave me new purpose. I am aware of the blueprint necessary for success. Hopefully, I have provided a blueprint for another successful sports agent or co-owner. We may eventually share a dinner table at Strip. I'll be the one wearing a Bnei Herzliya jacket.

SPORTS MANAGEMENT NOTES

What's NEXT for your career in

sports management?

1. WHAT will be the name of your sports agency?

2. WHO will you serve?

3. WHAT is your agency's mission statement?

4. WHAT services will you offer professional athletes?

5. WHERE will you be located?

6. EXPLAIN what sets your agency apart.

7. WHAT are FIVE steps you need to take to get started today.

WORKS CITED

MICHAEL, G. (2011). How to Invest in Sports Teams and Groups. In Investopedia. Retrieved from https://www.investopedia.com/financial- edge/1211/investing-in-sports-teams-and-groups.aspx

SHROPSHIRE, K., & DAVIS, T. (2008). The Business. In The Business of Sports Agents (pp. 22-36). Philadelphia: University of Pennsylvania Press. Retrieved from http://www.jstor.org/stable/j.ctt3fj0hr.6

Made in the USA
Coppell, TX
08 July 2023